Happiness in Your Life - Book One: Karma

Doe Zantamata

DEDICATION

For my Dad.

CONTENTS

i. Overview: What Karma is and What it is Not

The widest known definition of karma is "What goes around, comes around," or, what you do and say will come back to you, good or bad. This is actually only one of the twelve laws of karma, The Great Law (As you sow, so shall you reap). People generally use it in reference to someone acting in a really awful or really wonderful way. We let go of some anger towards mean people knowing that their karma will catch up to them. We root for those who always seem to be doing many nice things for others.

However, karma is not a reward and punishment system. Karma has a basis in understanding. If Person A does something good for Person B, they will not suddenly win the lottery. They will, however, be given a situation where they are able to take on the perspective of that person that they did the good thing for. Person B's karma is also affected, and they will be given a situation where they can choose to take the role that Person A did before. Whether they choose to do something good, or "Pay it forward" or not, is entirely up to them, but will affect both their karma, and the person they choose to do good for or not.

In this way, karma is a completely connected series of events between ever growing numbers of people. If you wanted to start a business when you were 25, and someone lent you money to do so, this would be an example of an event that may not catch up to you until years later. It may be that your business took off and you were very successful, then at the age of 55, someone approached you with their business idea asking for money to help make it happen. This is your turn to have the perspective of the person who helped you 30 years before. Until that point, you may never have known or even thought about what their thoughts were when you'd asked years earlier. At this point, should you choose to lend them money, you've instantly set the course for them to become you in several years time. Should you choose not to help them, they will remember years later that you chose not to when they are approached. They may then choose to do as you did, or to do as the person before you did.

So from the outside, if a person is expecting to see any kind of punishment in this case, they mày be disappointed. By not paying it forward though, Person B has not changed anything for Person C. Person C, years later when in that situation, may even be MORE inclined to help a Person D with their business venture, because they KNOW how much of a struggle they endured without help. Or, they may take on an egotistic attitude that they pulled themselves up by their own bootstraps, so why should they help anyone else.

This is not only in business deals, but in all sorts of relationships. Cycles of parents and children go through this in both positive and negative ways. When a child learns from their parent, they believe

100% that this is how things are. They may grow up believing things that just are not true, and then unknowingly pass those things down to their own children. If this is a bad cycle, such as alcoholism or abuse, the adults always have the choice to break the cycle when it comes to their own children.

Breaking a negative cycle will not just affect those children, but all the next generations to come. What you do today can affect people hundreds of years from now, whether or not they even know of your name or that you ever existed. We're much more powerful than most of us realize, and our choices can affect hundreds, if not thousands of people.

Have you ever seen a generational photo? Where one set of great grandparents have all around them their children, grandchildren, great grandchildren? If they had 4 children, and each of those children had 3 children, and each of those children had 2 children, there are now 24 people who are affected by the choices they made and the things they taught to their children. We can see how over hundreds of years of family lineages, there is an ever increasing number of

people who pass down teachings just like heirlooms to
the next generations.

The start of this is awareness. Once an adult begins to
think about beliefs they have, and examine what
effects they have on themselves and others, they can
begin to correct beliefs and actions that give negative
results. Often times, parents will be a little shocked to
hear themselves say to their children things they used
to hear as children. This is awareness of karma, and it
is in these moments that people can reevaluate if those
words they are passing on to the next generation are
true and good or not.

Good karma increases people's connectedness and
collective good. Bad karma isolates people and results
in a more self centered collective.

Those who are Christians have no doubt heard, "Do
unto others, as you'd have done to you." This is also
The Great Law of karma, just worded differently.
While this statement is generally used to encourage
people to be good to others, the other meaning of it is
often not realized. It means also to treat yourself as

well as you'd treat other people. Don't treat yourself worse than you'd treat anyone else. When you give and do all the time but never accept when others try to give to you or do for you, you're depriving yourself of good things, and depriving others of being able to feel the great way you do when you give.

Receiving good with gratitude is not selfish at all when in balance with giving with an open heart. Not receiving good can also cause resentment.

For example, if you don't have much money but loan someone money to pay their rent, and then they do not pay you back but go out and buy a new sportscar, chances are you'll resent them for that. But it has nothing to do with them. To them, you're a very kind and giving person. They would be shocked to hear any negative comment come from you, and may even ask why you loaned money to them when you didn't have enough for yourself.

Then, what was thought to be "good" turns out to be a negative experience for both you and that person. This is doing unto yourself less than what you do for others. Eventually, you'll wonder why you do so much but have nothing to show for it, when truth is, you've done that to yourself. You wouldn't wish that on any person you care about, so do not treat yourself so poorly.

Keeping the flow of giving and receiving good is essential to building good karma, both for yourself, and for all those you come into contact with, and all those they, in turn, contact.

Let's move on to the 12 Laws of Karma. These Laws have been formed and passed down over thousands of years, and are thought to be of Hindu origin. If you are of one particular religion and are hesitant to read further, there is nothing to fear. Each of the religions makes many hundreds of mentions to these Laws of Karma, even if they do not separate them into any set of Laws or call them by that name. You may be reminded of certain passages from religious scriptures when reading the Laws. Karma is discussed in many religious and spiritual texts, including The Bible, The Qu'ran, Hindu and Buddhist writings. These passages are not "copying" Hindu texts; they are just another way to communicate the Universal Laws to all people. The Hindus did not make them up either. They were just the earliest known who have documented them.

1 THE TWELVE LAWS OF KARMA: LAW ONE – THE GREAT LAW

The Great Law of Karma is the one that all of the others basically boil down to. If you know no others but this one, it can guide you to a better life through building good karma. The others are situations or circumstances which may interfere with this Law in its' interpretation. If the other Laws are not known or are misunderstood, people may believe they are acting toward building good karma, when in fact they are not.

The Great Law states, "As you sow, so shall you reap."

You have complete control over all of your actions, and absolutely no control over many of the consequences. Eventually, however all of your good actions will lead to good consequences.

Let's say you're a farmer, and you've bought a giant parcel of land. You work the land every day, planting seeds, watering, fertilizing, and of course waiting. The crops look fantastic. The day before the harvest comes in, a tornado flies through town and wipes them all out.

Your first reaction may be that you did all that work for nothing. You may think that life is unfair, or that this whole karma thing must be broken. This is because your expectation of that particular circumstance was that you would be rewarded with a bountiful crop for all of your hard work. The important thing to do here is to get out of that angry victim state of mind as soon as possible. Know that karma does always come through. You may not be able to see it today, you may not be able to realize it even in a few months, but one day, you will know why something that appeared terrible happened after you did everything right. It will have sent you down a different path than the one that you expected, and if you stay positive and believe in the Law, your results will be even better than you could have ever imagined.

So in the farmer story then, that the crops were destroyed. Insurance paid the farmer 80% of what his crop would have been worth at market value that day. Immediately, he's saved an awful lot of time harvesting and transporting the crops to take to sell.

Now he's probably a little disappointed he's only received 80%. He may feel he earned 100% and this is unfair.

Fast forward one week when he would have been at the mill with all his crops. Little did he know, the day before, another country reported enormous output of the same crop, and the market value suddenly dropped to 50% of what it was the week before.

You see in this scenario, the tornado ended up getting him an extra 30% from insurance than what he would have received in sale. The other farmers in the other country still made lots of money from their crops as they were so plentiful, so people still had more than enough to eat, and the insurance company still got their premiums from all the farmers, so the payout to the farmer with the tornado damage did not hurt them at all.

If you do all you can, and think positively, know that your good is on its' way. If something doesn't seem good at all, do not let it bring you down or convince you to do bad instead. It may not come in the form, at the time, or from the person you expected, but it will always come.

Sometimes, the only thing in your control is the way you react to something. There was a story in the paper about a man in Orlando who had been fired from a job five years prior. He went to his former office with a handgun, and shot several people. No one was critically injured, but he ended up going to jail for the rest of his life. He got stuck on that day of being fired, and blamed everything wrong in his life on that event. He decided to act in an awful way, and his karma immediately caught up with him. His freedom is gone for the rest of his days.

Now take another example of a man who was fired, Walt Disney. He was fired from his job at the Kansas City Star, a newspaper. They said he was not creative enough. Disney decided to pursue his dream of a theme park. He was turned down for loans by just about every bank he walked into, but eventually found one to invest, and Disneyland was born. Disney would never have had the time to do this if he was still at that job at the Kansas City Star. He went on to be successful beyond even his own wildest dreams, and later Disney bought ABC. ABC owned many other companies, including The Kansas City Star.

Neither of these men were victims or lucky. Both men made their choices day after day, and years later reaped what they had sown. If on the day of being fired, you'd have told either where they would be in a few years, neither would have probably believed you.

Make certain of the direction of your thoughts and actions. They can either be destructive, or constructive. Both will eventually lead to a destination worlds apart from each other. Always stay in the constructive direction, and you will constantly build good karma. One day, it will all be worthwhile, even if only never having to regret being worse to anyone or at anytime in your whole life.

2 THE TWELVE LAWS OF KARMA: LAW TWO ⸱ THE LAW OF CREATION

The Law of Creation is just about identical to The Law of Attraction. It states that, "You attract what you are, not what you want." This follows also closely to "You can judge a person by the company he keeps," or, "Birds of a feather flock together."

If you look around you at the people you speak to and interact with the most, you can see yourself. While The Law of Attraction talks about energy and vibrational matches, some may believe this and others may not. They say that "like attracts like" in people and in all of nature but magnets of the same polarity repel each other.

More likely, to look at nature, you could say that opposites of strong polarities attract, whereas those who are balanced do not attract either of those polarities quite as strongly.

Say for example you are a woman with a very strong mothering instinct. You want to do your best in every relationship, and always be very supportive and appreciative. When it comes to romantic relationships, you've not had much success. While you may question this, and say, "What more can I do??" The real question should be "What LESS can I do?"

Adults with mental and emotional health do not want to be mothered by anyone, especially not their girlfriends or wives. They want to feel independent, strong, and like they are giving and receiving.

The only men you would be able to attract would be men who are emotionally and/or mentally immature. Instead of giving you back the attention, care, and love you give them, they probably would be the least likely sort to ever truly appreciate your efforts aside from in words, and would probably lean more and more on you, the more you try to support and be good to them. After some time, your needs and wants would probably be completely overshadowed or have disappeared altogether, while all of theirs and more are met, and they still are not happy. They may even leave the relationship and find someone who they can take care of in some way, emotionally, financially, or otherwise someone who to you appears to be even more of a fragile mess than they ever were.

If you did not make your own needs and wants important, no one else will have either. You may wish to find someone who would treat you wonderfully, but you probably would not want someone to dote over your every sniffle. That kind of person would probably repel you in an instant, but you may not realize it's because you're so alike.

Many people throughout history are credited with saying you must "be" who you want in a romantic partner. If you take some time to write down all of the things you want in a partner, really examine each one and be honest with yourself. Are you, or have you been all those things? If not, were you more or less?

More is not always a good thing.

If the cookies are to bake for 20 minutes at 300 degrees, you wouldn't think they'd be made even better by cooking them for 60 minutes or at 450 degrees, right?

Though the initial thought may be that you just can't find the right person, or that you're "too nice," it may be just that you're trying too hard and denying yourself too much.

Remember the reverse meaning of the first Law that you want to always be as good to yourself as you would be to anyone else. If you are not good to yourself, the only people you will be able to attract and keep in your life are those who are not good to you either.

If you make yourself into a doormat, people will walk all over you. No one will ever treat you better than you treat yourself. So treat yourself well, and others will soon follow. Maybe not the ones who are in your life right now, but they will leave, and others who are kinder to you will soon take their place.

This may be a hard habit to break for chronic givers. They may have forgotten what it is to accept and receive with grace. Awareness is always the key to transformation. If you are a chronic giver and do not like to accept anything, even just the act of becoming aware of what you are communicating to the world will give you insight. The next time someone attempts to give you a gift, or pay you a compliment, accept it with grace. Even if you have to force yourself to do so because it feels so new and awkward, do so. It will become easier. Your habits of non-acceptance are actually the incorrect response, because it discourages people from doing nice things for you or treating you well. If someone gives you a compliment, even if you feel it's too kind or not deserved, just say thank you. They mean it. By not saying thank you or denying it, you're creating a negative experience which was not their intent.

The next time someone gives you a gift, again, accept with grace. There are some who just refuse to accept a gift and are so adamant about it that they will convince the giver to never ever give to them again. Denying a person's appreciation towards you will literally cause fewer and fewer people to appreciate you. Those who do so will do so less and less, and will come to expect that you do more and more. They are not bad people, but eventually you will convince them that this is what you truly want.

If you want to improve your relationships and circumstances, don't focus on trying to change the people around you. Instead, focus on yourself. Become the person who you want to see all over your world.

3 THE TWELVE LAWS OF KARMA: LAW THREE – THE LAW OF HUMILITY

The Law of Humility states, "What you resist, persists for you." This Law is one of the shortest as one line, but has many layers of meaning and examples in our current time.

Most people know what it is to be humble. It is being grateful for deserved appreciation, but never boasting about achievements or superficial things.

Some people, however, take "being humble" too far, and refuse to accept any sort of attention or compliments. This is actually just as bad as boasting.

Each of us has been given gifts and talents. Our combinations of gifts are unique to us. Though we may look at others and think we may never be "as good as" they are in something, or that "we're better than" someone else in something else, those comparisons really do not have anyone's best interest in mind. It's kind of like saying, "That grand piano will never drive as fast as that sports car." Well of course it won't, it wasn't designed for driving. It was designed to play beautiful music. Rather that feeling blue about what we do not have or who we are not, we can learn to appreciate what we do have and exactly who we are. It just requires a shift of focus.

If your passion and talent is in one area, even if the area doesn't seem to be practical, it's important that you develop your talent and enjoy it as much as you can. People around you can benefit from it, and most millionaires and billionaires were made because they had a passion for a certain thing and a career or business formed around that passion.

The world may not need another chef, or another party planner, or another actor. But the world really doesn't need another anything. There are plenty of people to fill all the roles in society. What the world DOES need, is more passion and joy. When you love doing something, and you share it with people around you, the joy is contagious. You can inspire other people to get more active in what they love doing, whether it's the same as you or not. To use your gifts and celebrate them is an incredible display of humility as it shows that these gifts are appreciated and were given to the right person.

In this way, "What you resist" was your gift, passion, or something you always wanted to do. It "persists" in your life in that it will always be an interest, you'll always wish you would do more with it, and one day, when you are grey, you'll regret not giving it a try.

Another meaning of humility is in extending that to others for their passions. If a person is really passionate about something, often they are criticized for a variety of reasons. The people who criticize are no better than bullies. They tell them something is foolish, or a pipe dream, or not practical, or just plain stupid. Sometimes they even claim to be trying to "help" the person by dumping all over their ideas, because they claim they don't want to see them waste their time or money, or they're just trying to be realistic.

Realistic is in the eye of the beholder. One person's reality is another person's pessimism. There are two kinds of people in the world: "Realists" and "Optimists." When you have a great idea, the "realist" will tell you 50 reasons why it can't be done, while the "optimist" will tell you to go for it and hope that you'll find the one way it can.

It's much easier for people to live their truths when they are encouraged. Even if something isn't for you, or seems like a silly idea, encourage a person to seek out their passions.

If you are seeking yours, listen carefully to those around you. If they constantly project negativity toward your ideas, just stop telling them about them. If you have no one who supports your ideas, then keep them to yourself until you find people who do, or who have similar ideas themselves. Two wheels attached together spinning in opposite directions will go nowhere, but two attached wheels spinning in the same direction will go twice as fast. When you share ideas with people, you are attaching your energy to them. Remember that.

The third portion of The Law of Humility deals with this as well, but in a slightly different way. On the positive, good karma building, it's speaking well of people when they're out of earshot. On the negative and bad karma building, it's known as gossip.

One of the greatest compliments about a person is that they never have a bad thing to say about anyone. This is a person you know you can trust, and one who always attracts good energy and allows people to be themselves without worry of being criticized.

Why then, do so many people gossip? Gossip is a result of pride and low self esteem. People talk poorly about others in order to feel better about themselves. But this never makes them feel better about themselves. Being a better person would make them feel better about themselves and raise them up, but that may seem a scary, vulnerable thing to do, so they try to bring others down with their words instead.

When you gossip, you are spreading something that may or may not be true (no matter who or what the source), and if you put your word on the line to whoever you tell. If enough people say something enough times, even if it's found out to be untrue, they have it so deeply in their minds at that point that they still believe the false gossip over the truth. At that point, they internalize it and are more determined to be "right" about the gossip they spread, than to see things how they really are.

The old adage, "If you don't have anything nice to say, then don't say anything at all," was introduced to us when we were in grammar school, and we should do our best to remember it. Gossip is hurtful, painful, and what's worse, with the Laws of Karma, anything you put out there will come back to you ten-fold.

If you tell someone some gossip, even if you believe it to be true, you will, without a doubt, be gossiped about soon afterward. The person or people who gossiped about you will also believe something to be true, and tell others, possibly thinking they're doing the right thing to "warn" them of you.

Unless the rumor is that someone is a chainsaw wielding animal, no one really needs warning, do they? If someone is nice to you, and you enjoy their company, that's who they are to you. If they just don't get along with someone else, that has nothing to do with you, and is not representative of "the kind of person they are." There may be other reasons which you know not of.

The more a person participates in gossip, the less trusting they become of people in general, and the more negative karma they build. Our entire justice system is based on being innocent until proven guilty, yet our entertainment, a lot of the nightly news, reality shows, tabloids, are based on being guilty on a shred of rumor, and who cares if they're actually innocent or not.

One of the items in The Optimist Creed is, "I promise myself to give so much time to improving myself that I have no time to criticize others."

This was written around 100 years ago, but it definitely holds true today.

If you don't bother yourself with gossip, you have only the most wonderful things to talk about, and all the time to do so. You can have conversations that actually make you feel good when you are done, and spread positive energy into the world.

That energy will also come back to you ten-fold.

If you think of people in your life who start out most conversations with "Did you hear?" you'll likely know them to be pretty unhappy in their own lives, moving from one drama to the next. By not engaging in gossip with them, you can actually help them to become happier by giving them something else to talk about.

Wouldn't that be a wonderful goal? To have every conversation lift each of those involved up instead of bringing the one who's not involved down? Be aware of your words about others and make it a point to stop yourself whenever you begin to gossip no matter how true you think it is.

The fourth portion of the Law of Humility is that resisting how things are actually creates more resistance. What you put your focus on, grows. What you don't put your focus on, shrinks. Have you ever heard, "Out of sight, out of mind?" We can extend that to "Out of mind, out of life." If you are tired of this or fed up with that, stop talking about and thinking about how tired and fed up you are. Otherwise, you'll continue to see more of the same, in the same people and in different ones. Focus instead on what the opposite is what you would rather see.

For example if you're tired of seeing that pets are in shelters, instead of getting angry about this or protesting shelters, think of the opposite. The opposite would be that more pets are getting rescued. Volunteer with a rescue, encourage others to adopt pets instead of buying them. Pretty soon, you will not only be accomplishing saving of animals, but you will inspire others to do the same.

What you resist, persists. The energy of something that you don't want cannot be cleared or changed by you expending more of that same energy. In order to see more good, you must do more good.

4 THE TWELVE LAWS OF KARMA: LAW FOUR – THE LAW OF GROWTH

"Wherever you go, there you are." This Law basically states that we create our own surroundings. As stated previously, we make all of our choices, but we cannot choose all of the consequences.

Real and lasting change within a person comes in tiny increments over long periods of time. If you are a person who strives to be the best you can be in all areas of your life, then you will look back years from now and be able to see how much you've grown and evolved into a happier, healthier person with a lot more love in your world.

If you keep making the same choices, you'll keep having the same results good or bad.

This can be seen in relationships, a person's health, at work, and even financially.

Everyone knows someone who goes from one awful relationship to the next. Though the person may seem wonderful at the start, they become the same person as the last bad relationship over time. This ties in closely with the Third and Fifth Law.

If a person chooses to just end a bad relationship and leap into a new one, no growth has occurred. This is why that relationship will become the same as the previous one.

If you give a person with a low money mindset a big lottery win, or sudden fame and fortune, they'll soon be flat broke again. There are stars and athletes who have earned tens of millions of dollars and somehow spent it all within just a few years.

If you took a person with a great work ethic, one who used their talents and passions which they had already developed, and one who knew how to manage money and had made themselves a millionaire, you could take all of their money away and they'd manage to have it all back and then some in a relatively short amount of time.

Some people go from one job they love to another job they love more. This is also not just luck, but that person creating and recreating and improving their environment, based on the improvement they have going on within themselves.

Gastric bypass surgery has been a lifesaving wonder for some, but for many others, they end up gaining all the weight back that they lost. The ones who succeed in keeping the weight off and staying healthy changed their mindset about food and exercise, and dedicate their choices every single day towards their health. The ones who gain everything back may have had initial success because they literally could not eat, but over those tiny increments of time, they slowly ate a little more and a little more, and skipped the workout and the walking, and their stomach stretched and the weight came back on.

Every single day holds opportunities for growth. If you're seeing something negative persist in your life, picture a goal of what you'd ideally like that picture to look like instead. Keep that picture fresh in your mind daily, and make choices that are in the direction of that picture. If something, or someone, does not fit into that picture, then put your attention instead on someone or something that does instead.

Educate yourself on those who have already achieved the full realization of that picture. Whether in business, love, or even just as a person, many people who have achieved a great deal in their lives want others to do the same. They write autobiographies and tell people about the struggles and inner demons they faced, and how they overcame them.

No one is just lucky in life, and no one is just unlucky in life. Though all of us have moments of sheer luck or unexpected calamity, for the most part, our lives are all our own doing once we reach adulthood.

Do and be your best in every day, and you will continually become a better person. Compare yourself only with yourself. You don't know others' full story, and there's no need to feel guilty for not being as good as them, or feeling justified in being "better" or "worse" in any area. We all walk our own path, and we all have our own lessons and challenges to face.

The more you focus on you, the better you will become.

Those negative relationships in your life, or possible future ones, you don't even have to forcibly remove once you focus on yourself. People will only treat you the way you allow yourself to be treated. If a person has control issues, they only want to be around people they can control. If a person has self esteem issues, they only want to be around people they can talk down to who will take their verbal abuse.

These people can be bosses, coworkers, friends, or even family. These negative types of people cannot stand to be around people who have a healthy self esteem, or people who are confident in their self-worth. The more focus you put on yourself to discover your own beauty, strength, and talents, the more they will not be able to stand being around you.

They may even become even worse to you, or accuse you of being egotistical or full of yourself, or "out of line." There is no need to argue, as for them, this is their truth. To them, you are only a projection of what they believe in their world. If their world is full of mistrust or anger, nothing you can do will please them for very long.

You may be fired, you may lose some friends (who were not truly good friends anyway), or your spouse may leave. While no one is 100% comfortable with change or what's perceived as "loss," you cannot change another person. You can only change yourself. If they were a cruel and belittling boss, they'll soon be a cruel and belittling boss to someone else. By letting these people go from your life, you're creating a space that can be filled with people who treat you better. By continually focusing on yourself, believing in yourself, and recognizing and appreciating your own self-worth, the only people who will be able to be around you long term will be the ones who feel the same way.

5 THE TWELVE LAWS OF KARMA: LAW FIVE – THE LAW OF MIRRORS

The Law of Mirrors is very similar to the previous two Laws. It states that, "Whenever there is something wrong, there is something wrong in us."

This is The Law of Personal Responsibility.

The Law of Humility was about becoming aware of who you are and how you treat others. The Law of Growth deals with taking that awareness and committing to becoming better and better throughout your life to recreate your environment. The Law of Mirrors shows you how to gauge your progress, and what is still left that needs improvement.

Our world is just a reflection of all of our beliefs about ourselves, others, and how things work. We're only given one perspective in this life, and that is our own. There are close to 7 billion people on this Earth, and if you asked each one to write down their thoughts about people, circumstances, health, and themselves, you'd get 7 billion different answers. To each person, this would be a true reflection of how the world really is, and they would not completely agree with anyone else.

Your world can be heaven or hell, depending on how you view yourself, people, and events. A homeless person with a cat for a best friend may actually be happier than one of the wealthiest people in the world who has thousands of acquaintances. While we cannot enter the minds of anyone else on this planet, we can decide to look at our own lives and be grateful for everything that is good in them.

If there is something wrong in our world, there is something wrong in us.

To a person who wants to be world famous, being an unknown is a curse. But to famous people who are private by nature, the fact that their personal lives make the nightly news, or that they're followed by photographers everywhere they go is a nightmare.

You may not want to have a house bigger than 2 bedrooms, and you may not want to get married and have children. To your parents, they may look at your life and try to encourage you to do or be things that they think will make you happy. Society may show images or provide pressure to be or do certain things. But if something makes you happy that is not what makes 99% of the people in the world happy, neither of you are right or wrong in your thinking for anyone but yourselves. Encouraging people to live their own truths is a great gift. Encouraging others to live your truth is a huge burden.

If your romantic relationship is unfulfilling, it may be habit to try to change that person into one who fulfills you more. But that's like noticing a spot of chocolate on your face in the mirror, and wiping the mirror for hours or days trying to remove the spot. Only by changing yourself, or by cleaning your face, can the mirror reflect the change.

By continually changing yourself, your world will continually reflect the change.

If your friends enjoy a round of poker and some beer every weekend, but you're tired of it, it would be much easier to find other friends who enjoy what you enjoy, rather than to try to convince all of those other friends to stop doing what they enjoy doing just because you don't enjoy it anymore.

If you suddenly develop a passion for photography, your family may not be quite as interested in looking at a few hundred photos of the park as you are. But there are plenty of other people who share that passion, and you may even run into some of them while taking photos at the park.

As you allow flow and change to occur, and as you keep looking inward, letting go of situations that cause you grief, and increasing the time spent in situations that allow you to be happy, your world will change.

It may change subtly or slowly, or it may change drastically. This is all just a direct reflection of your inner world.

No person or people are to blame for everything bad in your life, and no person or people are the sole cause of everything good in your life. Remember, wherever you go, YOU are there. You enhance or detract from all of those people's lives as much as they do to you.

If it's a chronically angry friend, and you hang around and listen to them complain, you're not helping them. Until they have no one left to complain to, they will continue to do so. Only when there's no one else to listen, will they be able to see that this probably isn't the best way to live.

Any award winner who gets up on a stage immediately has a list of people to thank. But all those people also have that person to thank for their success as well.

When we remove fault or blame, we are more able to see what we can do to create change. If you blame someone for "making" you unhappy, you're leaving it up to them to change before you allow yourself lasting happiness. They may not change in their entire life, or they may change, but only temporarily. When you accept responsibility for your life, you are literally taking control of your own destiny.

Who do you want to be? It's up to you, and only you, to make it so.

The other part of the Law of Mirrors is that by viewing the people in our world and the corresponding labels we give them, we can see what is going on inside of us. When you are able to label something, it means it's in you. If you are unable to label it, it means that it is no longer within you.

For example, a person who has been treated poorly all their life, if a kind person comes into their life, they will be stunned initially by the kindness. It's foreign to them. They may question it, or try to label it, or question the person's motives for the kind acts.

An ancient Shaolin saying is that "One cannot give what they do not possess; one cannot possess what they have not been given."

If you act kindly toward someone who has never had that experience before, or at least not in their recent memory, this kindness may not be returned to you by them. But it will one day be given to someone else by them, because of you. And kindness will be given to you by them, or someone else, and many others, as long as it still remains in you.

This is why it's important to not isolate one unreturned gift, whether it be kindness, compassion, generosity just because the one who you extended the

HAPPINESS IN YOUR LIFE - BOOK ONE: KARMA

great gift to didn't return it, it in no way means it won't be returned. If you allow their non return to make you bitter, in other words say, "I got burned once, never again," or "I was used once, never again," then you have made yourself a worse person because of that interaction, and you will be a worse person in all of your future interactions until you let that go.

This is common with the unwanted gift of mistrust. If a person dates another and trusts them fully, and that trust is broken, say by lying or cheating, the person may feel the need to protect themselves from any further pain by not trusting anyone anymore. But as soon as they make that decision, they will repel anyone who is trustworthy, and the only ones they will be synchronized with are those who also do not trust.

If we can label a quality in another person, then it means that quality is also within us.

This can be good or bad news!

Think of the people you know, and think of or make a list of the qualities you would say they have. Be honest. This is just an exercise for you.

49

Some people, you may describe as kind, generous, thoughtful, or others you may say are arrogant, self-centered, or inconsiderate. All of the qualities on your list are also in you. This is at first difficult to believe, as when we're calling someone arrogant, we certainly don't think we are, too.

Whatever you believe about someone, they probably also believe about you.

Have you ever been told you were so thoughtful by someone who you believe is very thoughtful? Have you ever been called controlling by someone who you believe is controlling? Or insecure by someone you think is insecure?

In all of those cases, you're both right.

This isn't an article intending to insult anyone or make anyone go on the defensive. This is an amazing shift in awareness that allows you to see the truth about yourself, as well as free you from other people's perceptions that you cannot change. It's a tool to help you make improvements where necessary, and also see what great qualities you have that you may not even realize.

A mirror will not show your beautiful hair if you do

not have beautiful hair. It will not show your large feet if you do not have large feet. It will not show any negative qualities that you yourself do not have, and will not show any positive qualities that you do not have, either.

This Law, when fully understood, also can also really help you understand why some people act the way they do.

Have you ever had a conversation with someone, a person you just met or even an old friend or family member, and you seem to be speaking two different languages? Maybe they suddenly get angry or accuse you of something or insult you, and you're totally taken off guard and shocked.

This is what happens when two mirrors do not reflect the same things. If they have within them something that you do not have, they see it in you even though it's just not there.

If you truly do not have it, you do not see it in them, yourself, or anyone else, because it doesn't exist in you.

When this attack happens, it's a really jarring experience. You may try to even clarify what you meant by something, but they still can only see what's being reflected back to them.

You may then ask another friend what they think of what's happened, in an attempt to try to figure it out for yourself. If that friend immediately says, "Oh, she's so " it means that friend recognized it, which means he or she also has that negative quality.

You may still not see it, and say, "I don't think so " no matter how certain they are.

Now, if that friend were also really confused as to why the first one blew up, then it means he or she does not have that quality either.

There is a danger in being close to someone who has negative qualities that you do not possess. The danger lies in your taking their blow ups personally and feeling awful as a result. When we're faced with something confusing like that from someone we love, it really hurts, and we sometimes internalize that pain. You don't know why they're so upset or angry, as you cannot see what they see, but you don't want them to continue to be upset.

What you need to realize is that there is nothing YOU can do to remove that negative quality from them. You can't even see it. It will be up to them to remove it from themselves. This may or may not happen in their entire lifetime.

If this is something that happens regularly, then you are setting yourself up for verbal abuse as long as you stay close to them. You can choose to put some distance between yourself and them, or if it happens weekly or even daily, you may even consider letting them go from your life.

By staying close to them and continually getting accused of negative qualities in your attempt to help them to not be upset, you may try so hard to understand and see what they are talking about, that you end up picking up some of those qualities. Then you would be able to clearly see those qualities everywhere you go, but it would also unfortunately mean that they've developed in you. This is not a good solution, and will decrease your overall happiness, and the happiness of everyone you contact.

Suddenly, you may see negative things in other people that they do not possess, but the qualities have become part of you, so you just see them everywhere.

Anger and confusion are actually your friends here. They indicate when there is a difference in mirrors.

For example, if you are always doing thoughtful things for someone, and they never do a thoughtful thing for you, you may not understand why and get a little angry about it. It means that consideration is just not in them.

If someone gets angry with you and you just don't understand why, it means that whatever they are angry with you about is not the truth. It's what they see in the world, so it's true for them, but it's just not in you.

Examples of this are:

- when someone is shy but gets accused of being arrogant
- when someone is outgoing but gets accused of being obnoxious
- when someone is kind but gets accused of "only" doing nice things for ulterior or selfish motives

If you can label it, it's in you. If they can label it, it's in them. If you both can label it, it's in both of you, good and bad.

Remember, too, that we're all walking our own path. While you may be tempted to convince someone that your acts were truly just thoughtful or kind, or you may be really hurt when they accuse you of something negative, you just can't convince them that your motives were pure. It's like two people speaking entirely different languages attempting to understand each other, or like a person who has sight getting frustrated with a person who is blind because they cannot see what they see.

Once you learn this Law, it really clarifies a lot of people's seemingly odd behavior. It suddenly shows that their behavior makes total and perfect sense. We're all on our own journeys here. There are some people in your life that get under your skin and that you can identify negative labels. Look at those, really look at those. Once you see them within yourself and change them, they will disappear from your whole life and all the people and circumstances in it. It's totally worth the reflection and honesty with yourself. There's no need to feel bad about it, even for a split second. What you don't know, you can't fix. Once you know it and fix it, you will add much more to the lives of all those you know, now and in the future.

6 THE TWELVE LAWS OF KARMA: LAW SIX – THE LAW OF SYNCHRONICITY

This Law states, "Whatever you do may seem very unimportant, but it is very important that you do it."

Everything in this world is connected somehow. The theory of 6 Degrees of Separation states that you know everyone in this entire world through six connections or fewer.

You may not be aware of this, but it really comes into action once you decide to follow your true path, and pursue the things you want in your life your dreams. The more you immerse yourself in any one thing, the more people suddenly appear who are on similar paths, or who can help you towards yours.

In the physical world, there can be no beach without billions of individual grains of sand. There can be no ocean without individual drops of water. No one grain is any more important than any other, and no individual drop of water will be missed if it's removed. Each one adding its own contribution combines to make the whole.

If you want to have and maintain a loving relationship with your spouse, it's important to keep this in mind every single day. Always take the opportunity to say thank you, to give a compliment, to help with anything, and to show affection. Tomorrow's memories are today's actions. If you become complacent or take someone for granted most of the time, then they will not feel appreciated or like they are a priority. They may find others who appreciate them more, and spend more time with them. Sometimes when couples split up, the one who has taken the other for granted for years or even decades will become completely overwhelmed with regret, and attempt to make huge efforts to win that person back. But by the time the one has left, it is probably too late and a big waste of energy. They could have kept the one around for a lifetime with thousands of small gestures, but they chose not to. If a person has been one way for years or decades, and changes that drastically, unfortunately it's more likely that the change will not last. Habits are sometimes very difficult to break, and real and lasting change only comes in many tiny increments over long periods of time. This is sometimes a very confusing and difficult lesson to learn.

If you want to build a brick house, you don't start with a giant mass of bricks already in the shape of a house and say, "Good deal." You start with one brick, and then another, and another, and eventually you will have that house.

One walk or one salad will not make a person healthier just as one cheeseburger or one day off from the gym won't make them unhealthier. Again, it's that daily commitment and that daily little effort that will build the unbreakable result.

This is true also with everything in life. Just because you have an idea about something, it doesn't mean it's time for the payoff or reward. The idea is only the very first step. Adding to that idea more ideas, then actions, then more ideas and actions, will definitely lead to the payoff.

If you were to set out for a 5 mile hike, you wouldn't expect to do it all in one giant leap, all in one instant. The same is true for change and goals. Set your goal, and head toward it. As long as you're going in the right direction, over time, step by step, you will arrive. Enjoy each and every step. The end is really only the very last step, and is of no more value than any of the other ones along the way.

7 THE TWELVE LAWS OF KARMA: LAW SEVEN – THE LAW OF DIRECTION AND MOTIVES

"You can't think of two things at the same time."

When something goes wrong in our life, our thoughts immediately go to what has caused this to happen. They go to the past, and to a negative place. This is important to be able to reflect on what to do differently next time, but more important is to then get out of that place and move into a positive, "what can I do from this point forward?" state of mind.

No matter how much you regret, how angry or sad you become, your yesterdays will never return. The world of "should have" or "could have" or "if only would have" is a world of pointless suffering, especially if the person who should have acted any differently was not you.

Time and events in our lives are just as they are. We choose which side we wish to view of them. Sometimes, the only "bright side" to something is that it's over. That's still a bright side and a positive way to look at it. The more times we choose to see the bright side instead of the dark side, the happier our lives will be.

When you're dwelling in a past and negative space, you have no time to think about anything else. You can instead choose to shift your thoughts onto today, what you can do today, and what you will do tomorrow. You can look to see what the lessons were from any negative experience, and see that without that experience, you never could have learned. With that experience and lesson, you will never have to learn it again, so it will never show up again.

This holds true in health, personal relationships, and business.

Everyone meets with failures, things that are unfair, people who treat them poorly. The ones who cannot move past those things are the ones who become the victims. They are stuck in something that cannot be changed, and keep reliving pain that only actually exists now in their own mind.

As long as you are alive, you have the opportunity to change your life for the better.

Though it may be challenging to see positives at times, there are always positives to be seen. Life is not a series of ups and downs, but rather a series of ups and challenges or lessons.

If you say and mean, "next time, I will do it right," then you are enforcing this law, as well as The Law of Growth. Mistakes are only mistakes if you keep on repeating them.

If you've ever heard the expression, "Fool me once, shame on you. Fool me twice, shame on me," this is one version of what this Law states.

By holding on to that pain and resentment, the course of your life will be guided by it. If your trust was broken and you hold on to mistrust, there will be no hope for a trusting relationship. If you had money or an idea stolen from you, and you hold on to that fear of it happening again, you'll push away people who could help you realize your next venture or help you develop your next idea. You may then look back and cite that person or event as the reason why nothing else in your life worked after that. But the truth is, all those things in your life after that happened when that person was no longer around and that event was over. It was the holding on to the fear or mistrust that caused the negative spiral.

Forgiveness actually only means, "to let go of resentment toward a person or event."

It has everything to do with you, and nothing to do with anyone else. Some people say that it's difficult to forgive, or that they will try to forgive. These statements mean that their attention is still on that person or event, and forgiveness likely will not be possible.

A much easier way to forgive, is to forget about it as best you can for the time being, and go on with your life as positively as you can (remember the Third Law, what you resist persists). Eventually, you will look back and realize that at some point, that anger, sadness, or resentment must have just disappeared, because you just don't feel it anymore. Once you are happy with your life, there will not be room for those hurtful emotions. You will be able to say that this person or event led to another, which led to a realization, which led to this wonderful life you have now. Without that person or event, the course of action in your life would have gone a different route, and would not have ended up where it is.

Some people go as far as to say you should feel grateful toward that awful person or event, which is a bit of a stretch. You should however, feel very grateful to yourself, for your own strength and perseverance, and your friends or others who saw you through that time.

Here's a little "Depression-busting Meditation" to help shift thoughts from negative to positive. Brain training, so to speak:

Do you ever get into a funky mood? Maybe just one too many unlucky or bad things happen in a short amount of time and it just gets to you? Well, before that bad mood grows, try this walking meditation to lift your mood:

A walking meditation is different than one where you sit, kneel, or lie down with your eyes closed. In a walking meditation, you're fully awake, but you're consciously changing your thoughts and being aware of every moment.

When a few things go wrong, it's easy to get into a thought loop of what an inconvenience this or that is, or how much is it going to cost to fix this...but remember, what you focus on increases, so by focusing on something being bad, more bad will soon come.

Instead, walk around your home, and actively look at everything in it. Start the thoughts, "I love my..." and as you look at everything, whether it be your child, your dog, a book you liked on a shelf, your refrigerator, just keep repeating "I love my..." and go around and do a mental inventory.

Pretty soon, you'll see that you have a lot of love in your home, you have a lot of conveniences, and you have a lot of great things. You'll likely FEEL your energy and mood shift from a depressed one into an uplifted one in just a few minutes.

It may sound too simple to actually work, but it really does!

At the end of this walking meditation, make sure to include "I love myself...for being able to see the positive in any situation." Close your meditation with that, and enjoy the feeling of gratitude which lives inside you.

Whatever problems, things that broke, whatnot, there are, you'll either fix them or make do without them for awhile.

You'll get through it.

Whether you're angry or sad about it, or choose to focus on all the good in your life instead and keep your happiness alive is really just a choice.

Another part of this law is evident when it comes to relationships. In new relationships, people tend to focus only on the good. They believe they've met someone "perfect," Mr or Ms Right. But that's because they've chosen to only look at the good. This may seem positive, but it's really not as time goes on. People who do this often after break ups can suddenly remember all the things they were choosing to ignore, and instead of a list of why that person is perfect, they can now tell you a list of absolutely everything that was "wrong" with that person. This is why in relationships, it's best not to focus on either the good or the bad of the other person, but to focus on your own feelings when you're around them. If you always feel good, then it doesn't matter really if they're doing something you think you want, or something different. If you feel bad quite a bit, then it doesn't matter if they have all the best reasons or excuses, you'll know that this relationship isn't the one for you.

If you've ever seen two people discuss a political candidate, or two lawyers argue a case, you can see this Law in action. You would think they were talking about entirely different people, because one is only focusing on the good, and one is only focusing on the bad. What's true? The truth is a mix of both, but who they want to support or who they want to bring down is the cause of why they see what they see, and try to persuade others to see the same as they do.

Seek good, find good. Seek bad, find bad. Seek truth, find truth.

8 THE TWELVE LAWS OF KARMA: LAW EIGHT – THE LAW OF WILLINGNESS

"If you believe something to be true, then sometime in life, you must demonstrate that truth."

We all have certain values and ideals. This Law states that if we hold these to be truths as general statements, we will be placed in circumstances that will require us to act in the way that we have determined to be "right."

This gives us a chance to prove that we were not just full of hot air.

If you've ever said, "If I got the chance to " then you will get that chance, but maybe not under the circumstances you'd dreamed up.

If you've ever said, "How could anyone ?" then you will be given a circumstance in life that will allow you to know how anyone could.

This has been used in modern day as "be careful what you wish for, because you just might get it."

Karma, as you can see by now, is over and over again, above all else, about understanding. When you ask these questions, you are asking the Universe for an understanding of those situations. Remember, you are absolutely no better and no worse than anyone on this planet. What makes us succeed or fail in life is our series of choices and beliefs. Those choices were in our control, but the consequences are not.

This Law requires you to act and speak with compassion, or to recognize that you do not know all the details in any given situation that does not directly involve you.

This affects us most often in our judgments about people and situations where we do not know the entire story as we're not living it ourselves.

For example to say, "If I ever dated a man like that, I would appreciate him every single day," about a friend of a friend's boyfriend. The time will soon come then, when you have the opportunity to date someone like him, or even to date him! It's only at that point that you have called it upon yourself to stay true to what you'd said that you'd appreciate him or someone like him.

Maybe you and he would have a fantastic go, and live happily ever after. Or maybe you would see that although he appears to be very sweet around new people, he actually takes those he knows well for granted. Maybe he seems so generous to everyone else, but then "needs" to borrow rent money from his family or girlfriend every month.

You then may turn into the friend of a friend who didn't seem to appreciate this man, as you'd understand why she acted the way she did, and you'd make the same choices as she did in getting annoyed and then leaving him.

Other examples of this are in career, parenting, or any situation in life where you've thought, "If that were me, I'd be better."

Would you really be a better parent? Or a better boss? Or take better advantage of a once in a lifetime opportunity?

Recognizing this Law and understanding it leads to less and less judgment. You begin to realize that most often, you really don't know enough about many situations to make a judgment call. You cannot make a whole decision based on a little bit of information.

Court cases are often dismissed due to lack of evidence. Circumstantial evidence is not even admissible as 100% truth, and a person cannot speak about what another person told them about another person. That's just hearsay.

Our justice system was based on truth, and has many guidelines that it follows strictly to uphold the truth. They even ask people to tell the truth, the WHOLE truth, and nothing but the truth.

The WHOLE truth part is a struggle for some people. They do tell the truth, a little, they just leave out a whole bunch of details that might make them look bad or might make the other side look better. This is again something to be careful of when listening to real world hearsay, also known as gossip. If people have an argument and want you to agree with them, they may, even unintentionally, leave out details or not even be aware of details that the other person had issue with. From their recounting of the argument, if you agree wholeheartedly that "so-and-so is a jerk," you may be asking for that same scenario to show up in your life where you are in the position of "so-and-so," so you can see why he or she acted the way they did.

This is the Law in which hypocrites are made. You may know of someone who always talked about the virtues of marriage and would say, "How could anyone ever cheat on their spouse?" only to find out that they ended up cheating on their spouse. What they actually did was not so much hypocritical, but speaking out of theory rather than first hand knowledge. By making those judgments, they asked the Universe to give them a situation in which they would need to make a decision to cheat or not. They then realized what made the other people who they condemned cheat, and they made the exact same decision that those others did.

When you realize and witness this Law all around you, you'll more than likely adopt a new stance about things you see or hear but do not know the whole story.

When a person comes to you with a wild tale about how awful or evil someone is, you'll be more likely to not participate in the "burn the witch" mentality, but rather say, "Well, we don't know the full story." Or "We don't know all the details." And leave it at that.

By not making judgment calls, you're also displaying two things; compassion and positive thinking. You're assuming that for a person to do something awful, they must have had a reason, and that people are all good inside, they just make bad choices.

What does this accomplish? It restores your faith in humanity. It builds your trust and shifts your reactionary way of thinking to one in which you ultimately believe all people are good, rather than that many people are bad, or evil.

When situations arise, you'll be able to halt others in their tracks when they assume the absolute worst about someone. You'll be able to interject some sense and prevent them from completely condemning a person who more than likely does not deserve it. You'll be able to possibly stop them from making a really bad judgment call on someone, which as you now know would result in them also living that same really unpleasant experience. Or maybe you won't be able to stop them, but you'll at least be able to warn them so that when they are living it, they can remember that they've brought this on themselves.

The world around you is only a reflection of what you believe to be true.

Now, if you believe and think things like, "it's too good to be true, easier said than done, or there must be a catch," you may think you're being realistic and not setting yourself up for disappointment. Actually, what you'll be doing is creating a belief system where those things BECOME true BECAUSE you believe them.

Then, when something really was almost too good to be true, would have been easier said than done, or when there was no catch, your belief system will be so much in conflict with it, that you will not accept, but will actually push away great things that didn't require and enormous effort or fight to occur. Those things that do come easily, you'll feel like "something's missing" but the only thing actually missing was the struggle, because you've convinced yourself that anything good only comes with great struggle.

You'll end up making life a lot harder than it actually ever needed to be. Before the outside world can change, your belief system needs to change. Then, the outside world will have no choice but to become an exact match to that belief system.

Your beliefs are the cause and the outside world is the effect, not the other way around.

No one and no circumstance can exist in your world without your permission.

If you believe the world to be a wonderful place, full of love and opportunities, people will show up, and circumstances will arise to prove those truths to you.

If you only WANT the world to be that way, but believe in your heart that it is not like that, the world will continue to show you only what you believe, and you will continue to want for better things.

The mind is a wonderful servant, but a terrible leader. Most of us operate in our daily lives by making our mind the leader. We see things around us, and respond with our feelings. Our feelings and what we see then create our beliefs.

This is opposite to how we have to operate in order to change anything that we don't want in our lives.

Our intuition is the leader, and the mind's job is just to follow the intuition. The mind is to be changed from the controller to the observer.

If you're at a place right now where everything just feels bad, then it's just a symptom of your mind being allowed to run the show for too long, and it did a bad job of it. Your intuition is telling you, this is all wrong. This is not how things should be. This is not how things have to be.

It's time to change your beliefs and let your intuition take over.

If your beliefs were shaped in your childhood, before you realized how the world really works, chances are, they were shaped with a lot of negativity. It's not your parents or anyone's fault it's just that they didn't know, and shared what they thought was true with you.

Now that you know, you can start changing everything immediately.

Keep in mind, that your daily beliefs have shaped your current world over a long period of time. Changing your beliefs is the start of changing your world, but some things may take a little bit of time. Some of your beliefs are so ingrained that they may really test you before going away.

Stay strong. Know and have 100% faith that this is true.

Every morning, and every night, take a few moments to reaffirm your super positive beliefs:

The world is a loving place.

People are all good inside.

You are worthy of everything great in the world.

Life is fun.

Life is an adventure.

Great things happen for you.

Though if you look at yesterday, or last week, or last year, you may be able to pick out "proof" that these things are not true, remember, that's just because your inner beliefs were not these things at the time.

Keep strong to these beliefs, and let your intuition be your guide. If something feels positive, or exciting, or just plain good, go with it. Your mind may tell you that things are too good to be true, or that you're being naïve or foolish, but that's just because it developed those habits and that is what's familiar.

Habits are changeable.

Try this take your computer mouse and move it to somewhere else on your desk. Or, move the garbage can in your kitchen to a new place. You will be really surprised at how many times you go for the mouse in the old place even though you know it's not there anymore. You won't believe how many times you toss something or almost toss something in the place where the garbage can used to be. Eventually, though, the new places, or habits, will become more normal and familiar.

The same is true for super positive thinking. If you decide to really believe those super positive beliefs, it will still take a little while before they become habits. Once they are habits, they will just become the way you think, react, and operate in your daily life. This is when things will really start to change for the better.

Now, nobody admits to being a "pessimist." Nobody. Even the biggest pessimists in the world will claim to be "realists." And it's true, that IS reality for them. It doesn't have to be reality for you.

Your job is to focus on yourself and your life. You don't have to prove anything to anyone or convince anyone of this. If they see the great big positive changes in your life, they will ask you what your secret is, and then you can tell them.

Affirmations for the 8th Law can help to be aware of positive beliefs and send them out into the world intentionally. They can be printed on paper, or said aloud...for example:

1. I trust my intuition and have faith in my decisions

2. I trust that all people are good at heart

3. I trust that even though I may not see it, the Universe is a good and fair place, and everything will work out for the best as long as I do my best.

Create your own set of beliefs and post them in a place that you can see them daily. They can be based on a religion, they can be something like The Optimist Creed by Christian Larson, or they can be entirely written by you based on your life experiences and beliefs you have and want to maintain no matter what individual circumstances seem to conflict with them.

Start today, believing in more positive and easier things, and the world will begin to reveal them to you over and over again.

9 THE TWELVE LAWS OF KARMA: LAW NINE – THE LAW OF BE HERE NOW

This Law states, "You can't go home again, but you must try."

"Home" does not mean that little apartment you grew up in on the East Side. Home actually means your emotional home the starting point when we were children, trusted fully, and believed everyone was good.

We all begin life as precious, innocent little beings. Some of us are bombarded with negativity at an early age in our homes. Some are bullied in school by the other kids. Some end up dating kids who are just plain mean. As we get older, we have many good experiences, but many bad ones, too. This is what Buddha referred to as "suffering."

We go from being innocent, to having these experiences, to then going one of two ways; either experienced, or bitter.

Bitter is another term for a person who has a whole lot of baggage from past relationships.

Holding on to negative experiences from the past brings them into the present. By keeping those bad experiences alive, you'll be asking for more of the same. You may end up dating people who are exactly like your mother or father was to you when you were a child. Children of alcoholics often marry alcoholics.

Reliving and dwelling on the negatives of the past, wondering what would have happened if things were different, prevents you from moving forward with your life. It prevents you from appreciating what you have now, and what you can have in the future.

Pretending the negatives of the past didn't exist completely, or burying them without a thought, can lead you to make the same mistakes over and over again without ever realizing why.

Reflection on the negatives past is necessary, because being removed from them allows you to have a different, more unbiased view of everything that happened. You can see what was completely out of your control, but more importantly, you can see what was actually in your control. You can then see what choices to make now and in the future to avoid recreating that same experience in your life. Doing this also allows you to make peace with those events, knowing that they are truly over, and that they were only a painful lesson that you've now learned and are free from ever repeating again.

You may end up choosing friends who bully you, or what they call "joking."

Why would people choose these types of relationships when they are free to choose to have only positive relationships?

Before we were bombarded with negativity, all we knew was love. We were curious, wanted to share things that we had, and felt no hesitation in telling people we love them.

How they treated us was what built our definition of how to love, or what love is. If we go through life unaware, we will keep recreating those negative circumstances in our lives. Once we become aware of things that were just not OK in our past or as children, we can decide to let them go and leave them in the past. We can then be free to live as we did when we were very young. We can then choose to only be close to others who will treat us well.

You can't go home again, but you must try. Your natural beliefs were to love, trust, be honest, and innocent of the "evils" of the world. All you knew was good. You were forthright with your wants and things you didn't want. Though you can never return to that innocence again, you can choose to let go of mistrust, pain, and all those learned negative things that are keeping you from being who you really are, and once were.

10 THE TWELVE LAWS OF KARMA: LAW TEN – THE LAW OF CHANGE

"The more things change, the more they stay the same."

You meet hundreds or even thousands of people in your lifetime, but only a few become close friends or romantic relationships. What attracts you to certain people goes back to the Law of Mirrors. What's in you is either in them, or the opposite is in them, creating a need to be close to them. If this need is pain based, it would be better if you were to realize it and be able to let it go.

Some people get married and have children early on, and others do not until later. Others never do. The ones who get married and have children early on will begin to become more like others who have gotten married and had children early on. The single ones will not relate to the joys and issues that the others have in their daily lives. Though they can still be friends, it's more likely that the married ones will gravitate toward married friends, and the single ones will find new single friends to spend time with.

This also goes along with The Law of Growth. If you're growing but your friends or romantic partner does not, eventually, you will "outgrow" them and have very little in common with them anymore.

Relationships in your life will keep repeating. If you've come to a place of self-confidence, self-worth, and happiness, you will keep on bringing relationships, work and personal, into your life that reflect these qualities.

If you are stuck in or have entered a place of sadness, despair, or anything else negative, relationships with those qualities will keep coming into your life and staying. This also goes back to the Law of Be Here Now. Adults often recreate themselves into their parents. Though they may have tried to become different in certain ways, or entirely opposite in others, they may have only succeeded in "flipping" that relationship.

If a person, let's call her Jane, was not paid much attention to as a child, or not given much appreciation, she may deliberately do the opposite for her own child. But polar opposites are not often good. Jane's own child may then always have had everything handed to him, never having to want for a thing. He may grow up to be very dependent on Jane, and then as an adult, still look to the her to provide everything for him, while never even thinking to return a thing. Jane then becomes that unappreciated child all over again, but in the role of the parent. Jane created this based on her beliefs. She will then pass on to her son the same set of beliefs, and he will seek out someone like her in his adult life.

Or if Jim had a father who was an alcoholic, he may decide that alcohol is not to be allowed anywhere near his home when he grows up. His children are told that alcohol is an awful, terrible, banned substance in their home. As they grow up, they see others who enjoy alcohol in moderation, and do not understand why something that's legal is so strictly prohibited in their home. Once they leave home, having never had the freedom to experiment with alcohol and learn for themselves that overdoing it will only lead to no good, they may go wild with it. They may themselves turn into alcoholics even in their rebellious teen years. Jim then becomes the victim of loving an alcoholic again. He may never understand that extremes lead to extremes. He may think alcoholism just "runs in his family" but that he was strong enough to overcome it.

Balance is key to most everything in life. If a person over or under does things, the opposite will appear in another relationship, creating a chain of dysfunction until someone along the line realizes it and makes a conscious change.

Under exercising can lead to poor health. Over exercising can take up so much time that there's not much time for anything else.

Overworking can bring money and material things, but also takes a lot of time away from family and friends. Not working at all leaves plenty of time for family and friends, but can result in a life of poverty and financial struggle.

To become the exact same as a well balanced parent is a wonderful thing. To become the exact opposite of an imbalanced parent usually leads the next generation to become the exact opposite of you, or, back to your parents.

Finding balance is no perfect science, and differs from person to person. One person may think that working 70 hours per week is the "right" amount, while another would quickly burn out after 40 hours per week. Both are right for themselves, but wrong for each other, and possibly others in their family. Becoming aware of your habits and beliefs and seeing how they match up with your family is key to avoiding disappointment and resentment and the polar flip.

This also plays in to how you are treated throughout your lifetime. If you carry with you low self-worth, you will find that people throughout your life, even ones who when you meet them start out nice, eventually turn into people who do not treat you well. The change must occur in you before it can occur in your life.

Time may pass, peoples' names and faces may change, but as long as you have the same beliefs, the more things change, the more they will stay the same.

11 THE TWELVE LAWS OF KARMA: LAW ELEVEN ⁃ THE LAW OF PATIENCE AND REWARD

"When you focus on your life, good things happen."

Abraham Lincoln said, "Whatever you are, be a good one."

What you focus on increases. If you look at your life and see all the things that you think you are missing, the material things, the prestige, you will see more things missing. If you look at someone else's life and see things they have that you do not, you will see more things that others have that you do not.

Comparison to others is like looking at the tip of an iceberg. Even if it seems like someone has it easier, luckier, has more good things going on than you, you really do not know the whole story. To try to find out more of someone else's story is also not a good idea, as it takes the focus away from what you have, who you are.

Imagine you were born in the poorest village in the world, to the poorest family. Imagine you were born blind, and with limbs that do not function. Imagine there is no food, no shelter aside from a shanty hut. Imagine living that way up until the age you are now. Now imagine being transported from that person's body into yours today.

That person may exist somewhere, and to be living your life, exactly as it is the way now, they would think they'd hit the lottery, or died and gone to heaven. You have SO much. If you're going to compare your world to someone else, why not compare it to someone else who has nothing, because surely there are people who exist who have nothing. You are so much more fortunate than you may realize.

Look at your life today as if you had been that person up until yesterday. From the soft bed in which you awake, to running water, power, food in the refrigerator, doesn't it now seem that every thing you

could have ever wanted in your life you now have?
Clean clothes to put on your back, shoes! Appreciate
every single thing, convenience that you touch. These
are just the material things! All the people in your
life, too, people who take time from their own lives
just to interact with you. And yourself, your beautiful
healthy self. The fact that you have access to modern
technology, you've had education, you've awakened to
a point where you can see things and appreciate them
as if they were brand new. A lot of people have all
these things or more but grumble their way through
life, never realizing how incredibly fortunate they are.
This alone, you can be grateful for, and thank yourself
daily.

As far as work, many people do not yet live in their
dream jobs. Movie director, star athlete,
photographer most people have a job which is secure,
good pay, not too many hours worked per week.

Back to Lincoln what he said should come as a
lightning bolt. No matter what your job is, do it as
best you can. If you work with people, speak kindly
and positively to them. Let every person leave your
presence just a little happier than before they arrived.

HAPPINESS IN YOUR LIFE - BOOK ONE: KARMA

There are a great many cashiers at grocery stores who do this. The job itself probably doesn't pay too well, and it's not exactly mind expanding work most of the time. But that few minutes spent ringing up each customer, a lot of cashiers will take the time to start up a little friendly conversation, and have each customer leave with a smile on their face. What a difference these people make! Sending hundreds of smiling folks out into the world. They probably make many people feel better about themselves and the world in just a few minutes, than years of therapy talking about what's so awful does in many years.

Not to knock therapy, there are plenty of great therapists out there. The ones who have the most success are the ones who use CBT. Cognitive Behavioral Therapy. What this does, is separates the circumstances from the person. The person is able to create a shield between themselves and whatever bad things come their way. The old expression for this is "Let it roll off you like water off a duck's back." When we let negative things stick to us, they eventually weigh us down. When we let negative things go, we have more room to appreciate positive things. What you focus on increases. This doesn't mean that nothing bad ever happens to the chronically positive. It just means that when bad things happen to the positive folks, they don't focus on what is so awful and what they cannot control or what isn't fair. Instead, they focus on what they can do to change things or make them better. This gets them out of the negative circumstances much faster.

Better to be excellent at an average job, than to be average at an excellent job.
Everything is temporary. We can only move in one direction; either constructive or desctructive. If you're just doing enough to get by, less and worse things will follow. If you're excellent at what you do, and always do your best, more and better things will soon come your way.

12 THE TWELVE LAWS OF KARMA: LAW TWELVE - THE LAW OF VALUE AND UPLIFTMENT

This Law is very similar to the First Law. It states that what you put in, you get back.

The difference in this law, is that it reflects on the whole. The First Law was personal, you will reap what you sow. This Law states that the great things you contribute are contributing great energy to the whole, and the negative energy you contribute also decrease the value of the whole.

If you look at certain neighborhoods, they may be run down. Litter and vandalism may be visible on every street. You may hear shouting or anger between families and strangers.

This is the collective. Some of these neighborhoods turn around. Usually, it's because of only a few people, who spark a change and inspire others to do the same. Those few people add so much value to the entire neighborhood, to the lives of every person who lives there now, and every person who will live there in the near future.

To maintain that positive energy may be difficult at first, but as it grows, so does the momentum. The initial one or few people can then look at not only their own lives for what they have sewn, but the lives of all the people around them who they inspired to sew better futures as well.

Certain people throughout history have awakened truth, freedom, peace, and compassion in the lives of millions. Mother Teresa, Gandhi, Martin Luther King, Jr, the Dalai Lama. In and of themselves, their lives may not be or have been much more opulent or fulfilled than many other people, but the value they added to the world and to millions upon millions of people is immeasurable.

Mother Teresa in her lifetime generated millions of dollars. She did not live in a castle, or drive a fancy sports car, but she continually distributed the wealth she brought in to increase the collective whole. To bring in a lot of wealth is not a materialistic goal. Self-centered use of extraordinary amounts of money is not wealth. Extraordinary amounts of money can be wonderful things when a person who generates them follows the Law of Value and Upliftment.

We sometimes feel as though we have to shun money in order to be spiritual. We hold negative beliefs about money, and think that those who have a lot of it are greedy. These beliefs limit us from doing more to better the world. Rather than reject money, we need to reject negative beliefs about money. Welcome it into your life and enjoy being able to help others because you have more than enough to live a comfortable lifestyle.

What you do for others around you, you do for yourself. What you do for others around you, leads them to do for others around them, which, like a boomerang, will end up benefiting you and those you love as well. We are all here for each other, and we all affect each other, whether we realize it or not. The more you do for the good of the whole, the better the world will be.

Those are the 12 Laws of Karma. Now, let's revisit them as they apply to relationships, judgement, and the world.

13 THE KARMA OF RELATIONSHIPS

We all have bad relationships. We all try our very best to win these people over and lose ourselves in the process. This is a lesson in self-worth. What we do from there, will dictate the rest of our lives. We can go from naïve to bitter, or from naïve to experienced.

If you choose to go from naïve to bitter, the next person you are with, you will treat as you were treated, hurt, may not even realize it. You may have been hurt because that other person never realized it because they were still stuck on someone else who was hurt by someone else. This is the karma of relationships. One who was closed off to you hurt you, so by closing off and being with someone else and treating them the same way, you can understand why the first one treated you that way. It had nothing to do with you, and it had everything to do with the fact that they should not have been in a relationship in that unhealed state of mind.

What to do? Break the cycle.

Don't date until you are ready, healed, have forgiven yourself for staying, and forgiven the other person for doing the things they did. How do you forgive? They were for some reason unable to feel compassion, unable to feel empathy. Maybe they had too low of self worth, or maybe too much fear, maybe they were still living in bitterness from the past all their actions towards you were based on those. Feel compassion for them that they lost you, that they will continue to hurt as long as they just don't see it.

Moving on.

If you've been hurt in a relationship really badly, you may want to build some walls around you so that it will never happen again.

You will then block 99% of the chance for broken trust, deception, lies, or anything else awful from ever happening to you.

But, if those walls are up, you will also block out 99% of the chance for trust, openness, truth, and love from ever happening to you.

Realize instead, that the pain was caused by THAT person, not every person. By keeping the walls up, you're choosing to punish yourself and every person who tries to love you.

Don't punish the innocent.

Improve your odds for love. Break down the walls.

What happens when you do not trust someone who is trustworthy? They tire of it quickly, and will not want to be around you. They are innocent and honest, and do not want drama, accusations, or anger directed toward them when they've done nothing wrong. This is why maintaining trust is so important. If you become skeptical and make people prove their trust to you, questioning their every move, you are going to chase away the very people you want to have in your life. We attract who we are, not what we want. If you are a person who does not have trust in their life, you cannot, it is not possible, to attract and keep people in your life who are trustworthy and trust others. They just won't stay around.

Don't date someone with baggage. They obviously don't realize it, but they are in no place to date. You don't want to be held accountable for the mistakes their ex made. It had nothing to do with you.

Trust, always, and you will be trusted. People who do tell lies can never keep them straight, so when you suspend judgement, you may hear conflicting statements but not jump to any conclusions. If you ask them why they've said two different things, they may get mad or overreact or ask you if you're accusing them of lying. Now, if a person has a good reason for two conflicting statements, they'll just give you that reason. If they go into a panic and ask you if you're accusing them of lying, it's likely because they are.

You can trust fully for the rest of your life, only knowing when people prove themselves to you to be untrustworthy. Those people do not have a place in your life.

104

Once you see one side of a relationship, Karma will allow you to see the other.

Always.

Now, if you realize this or not, is a different story. It may not be the identical actions or reasons, but the emotion underneath will be the same. If a man abuses a woman, he is exerting fear of loss through power. That energy, unless it's dissolved will be passed by her to someone else. Maybe her children, maybe her friends, maybe her parents someone will be on the receiving end of that fear of saying the wrong thing or else she will get angry, even though it's not their fault.

The courage to be alone.

Sometimes we think that we must find another immediately or that we wasted so much time with that person that we want to immediately get another person in our lives who is much better. This is a mistake. It is inconsiderate of the new person, and also is not allowing yourself the time to heal. Be patient with yourself. Solitude and reflection is not a lonely place. It's a place to become whole.

Give yourself enough time to heal. We aren't Tarzan here, jumping from vine to vine. Until you are fully over another, you should not date someone new. It's like bringing poison to the party. Even if you get through it, chances are you'll act mean based on fear in the beginning, then have to spend time trying to apologize, make up for, and amend your mean behavior to whoever sticks around.

One should not enter into another relationship before healing fully. Sometimes we end up punishing others for what exes did, then regret doing so, and subject ourselves to even more pain of regret of treating the new person poorly. We should be more patient with ourselves and allow enough time to heal before seeking a new love.

Stay aware of your feelings though, and don't let fear intrude when the time is right and when you meet someone new. Fear of not being with someone for so long may rise up and bring with it a sudden rush of any trace emotions. Squelch that fear, and act only out of love. Yes, love is a vulnerable place to be. Yes, you may get hurt again. However, once you make peace with those fears, you are free.

Work on yourself. Be aware of your motivations. Act only out of love.

With regard to self-worth, the lesson is that you don't need to put anyone else down in order to stand up for yourself. Standing up for yourself can be a calm, tactful act that you are comfortable with. You do have to stand up for yourself to keep from being put down, taken advantage of or taken for granted. We let people know how we will be treated, and they will only treat us as well as we project. This happens by both our actions, and by our inactions as well. Being non-confrontational is good, but shying away from confrontations that someone else started will only lead to more.

Remember in the second and third Laws, you attract what you are, not what you want, and what you resist, persists for you. Add to those the tenth Law, the Law of Change, and you will see that what you tell or don't tell people will continue you on this loop until the lesson is learned. By not tactfully asserting your self-worth, you are telling that person, and the world, "It's just fine to treat me poorly." So that person, and the world, will oblige your request.

Some may think that the mean people will face their own karma for treating people poorly, and that's true, but it has nothing to do with resolving their own. Those people will face their karma only when others do not allow their poor treatment. But to continually allow yourself to be treated poorly will not result in good karma for you, only in more and more people treating you poorly. Karma, remember, is not good or bad, reward or punishment, but understanding.

Those who allow themselves to be treated poorly will always see other people who those very same mean people treat very well. Without further examination, this may seem frustrating. "Why does he treat that person so well when that person does nothing for him, and yet he treats me like nothing when I actually make an effort for him and am nice to him?" Your answer is right there he treats that person well because that person has asserted that he will not be treated poorly. That person has his respect, while you and those who allow worse treatment, don't.

This confidence cannot be faked, but rather, will come in your every response and action once your self-worth is raised. By realizing your own self-worth, a detachment occurs, so that when another person treats you in a way that you don't like, you will not even be tempted to say, "It's OK," or "that's fine," or any other placating statement. Those statements do not cause them to appreciate how kind you are, but instead make them realize subconsciously that it's OK to do so again. In fact, by saying those things, you're literally telling them that is true.

High self-worth removes the need for approval. It also removes the need for everyone to like you. People with lower self-worth really need for others to like them, otherwise they feel found out, that those people see how awful they are. They then try to win over those people by being extra nice, which actually makes them into doormats for those people, who didn't even like them much in the first place and have no problem walking all over them. You can be a great person and have others just not like you much for no apparent reason. In fact, the reason may be that they're just not choosing to be great people themselves.

Keep your focus on you, and stay aware of what your words and actions to one person are really telling them. If something keeps going wrong, like a pattern, then the link to all those relationships is not "all men" or "all women," but rather, you. You can always tell a person who hasn't realized this yet. They are the ones who say, "all men are liars" or "all women are manipulators." We know this isn't true, but to them, not realizing their own responsibility in creating their relationships, it is true. And it will continue to be true until they turn their focus inward and make a change.

14 THE KARMA OF JUDGEMENT

Without knowledge of Karma and how it truly works, people may judge others, then have a negative situation occur in their lives and not realize how the two are connected, or what the lesson is.

Once understood, a person will likely never judge another again...if not for the other person, for themselves.

When someone appears to have done something "bad," it's best to suspend all judgement. You may have seen an action or heard some words, but you do not live in the mind of any other person, so you do not truly know the reason or motivation behind what they do. When you assign a reason, that reason says more accurately how you view them or the world at large, and may not be what's true at all. If you're positive and trusting, the truth may be much more sinister that you've deduced. If you're negative or mistrusting, the truth may be much more innocent than you have imagined. If you like a person, you're apt to give them the benefit of the doubt. If you don't like a person, or if you don't know them, you may more easily condemn them. Suspending judgement is the best practice.If an action or words have hurt you, speak up for yourself, and remove yourself if necessary, but don't extend it to judgements about them or their character. You may be way off.

If you can help a situation, do so, if you cannot, adding any negative thoughts and words to the situation will only cause it to grow and echo back to you.

If I wish it on you, I wish it on me.

Any angry thought or words you send out to another person, you are wishing upon yourself 10-fold.

Any positive or loving thought you wish onto another person, you wish upon yourself 10-fold.

Do you see why it's so important, not just for them, but for you, that you wish only loving thoughts to others?

So what if then someone has done something awful? What if your normal reaction is to condemn them or say they are a bad person? Then you are wishing for a similar circumstance to appear in your own life, one where you may end up making the exact same decisions they had.

Instead, suspend all judgement. Look to them and say, "That action has caused others pain. I wish you the knowledge to know that this is not a kind way to treat others. I wish you discover within yourself the empathy and compassion that you will never do something like that again, and that you will make amends as best you can for what you have done to that person."

Do you see the enormous difference?

In one, you feel anger. You direct anger outward, anger will come back.

In the other, you feel empathy, you direct out love, and love will come back.

When you see an action, or even an inaction, that's witnessing. If you attach a reason or motivation behind someone else's action which is negative, that's judging. Judging says more about your beliefs about another person or the world at large than it does about that actual person or the world in truth.

We tend to judge more people who we don't know or don't like. People we like, or love, we either give them the benefit of the doubt, or ask them what their reason was for doing something.

One of the most common little judgements comes when someone does not call or text back. The only thing that is known is that they didn't call or text back. Reasons may be attached like, they don't think you're important, they can't be bothered to call back, they must be out cheating, or all sorts of reasons that exist only in the insecurities of the person who is not being called back.

Judgement is what we've trained our minds to do, and

what we were trained to do in school. Use logic, connect the dots. So for most of us, it's not a matter of just not judging, but rather a matter or realizing when we are judging, and consciously deciding to suspend that judgement until more information can be gathered.

By doing so, you're actually giving everyone the benefit of the doubt, and preventing bad feelings from forming within yourself toward any person.

15 KARMA AND THE WORLD

Imagine if the world were to end every night and begin every morning. You'd have no regrets to hold onto and would make certain to make every day count. We all know we're going to die, yet we hold onto negative experiences that no longer exist, relationships that make us feel awful inside, and anxiety or worry over things that may never be.

Attachment prevents us from actively being aware of our Karma. We think of things like loyalty, really, really trying to help someone, or commitment to abusive people somehow as good things, but they are destructive to ourselves and to others. People sometimes need to fall in order to get up on their own strength. If you're constantly protecting someone, covering up their misdeeds, or enabling them to act in bad ways, you are not helping them. You are hurting them and others by delaying their rock bottom. Their rock bottom will be painful to watch, but it will be the only way that they can see they need to change. Delaying their rock bottom will actually make it harder for them, involve and hurt more people. We always want the best for people who we care about or love, but attachment prevents us from letting them go to be who they are going to be. We can't control that, even though we may wish they would just see and do things the way we know it would be better. Each of us has our own journey to travel and choices to make. Allowing someone to make those choices, and those mistakes, is not the same as causing them pain. They are choosing to cause themselves pain. Our only choice is if we allow them to cause us pain, too.

Every little thing you do matters. Every kind word you speak, every smile you share, every day you brighten, just by being you. Keep your life in such order that you are always able to be the best version of you that is possible. Stay close to and give attention to people who love you as you are, and who encourage you to be yourself. Love others as much as you love yourself, and care for yourself as much as you care for others.

All of the Laws of Karma can be simplified down to The Great Law: As you sow, so shall you reap. Every good word, thought, and action that you put out to the world will come back to you. For this reason, always, always do good and think well of yourself and others. Your world is a paradise waiting to be discovered but it must first exist within you, and it cannot exist without you. Choose to believe in great things, and act out of love, and love and great things will make themselves known to you, or form wherever you may look. Life is just one long series of interconnected moments, so find the joy in every moment, and you will find the joy in life.

Please visit happinessinyourlife.com

for information about other books

by Doe Zantamata.

May you find peace in your heart,

And joy in your life,

Always.

Made in the USA
Lexington, KY
07 September 2014